PIANO . VOCAL . GUITAR

CHART HITS

2015-2016

WITHDRAWN

ISBN 978-1-4950-5225-5

HAL•LEONARD®
CORPORATION
7777 W. BLUEMOUND RD. P.O. BOX 13819 MILWAUKEE, WI 53213

Visit Hal Leonard Online at
www.halleonard.com

ADVENTURE OF A LIFETIME

Words and Music by GUY BERRYMAN,
JON BUCKLAND, CHRIS MARTIN,
WILL CHAMPION, MIKKEL ERIKSEN
and TOR HERMANSEN

Moderately fast

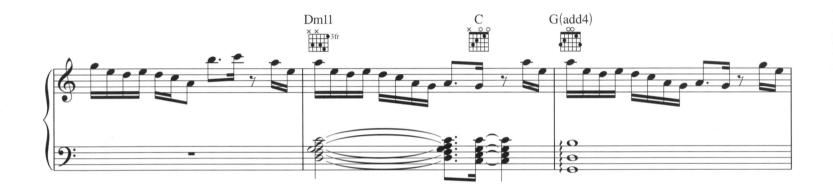

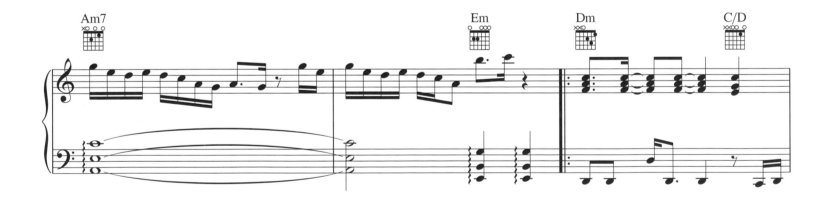

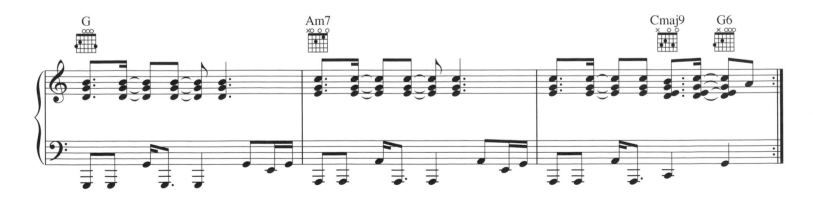

"Turn your mag - ic on ____ for me," ____ she'd

say. "Ev - 'ry - thing you want's _ a dream a - way. ____

____ Un-der this pres - sure, _ un - der _ this weight, we are dia-

BURNING HOUSE

Words and Music by JEFF BHASKER,
TYLER SAM JOHNSON and CAMARON OCHS

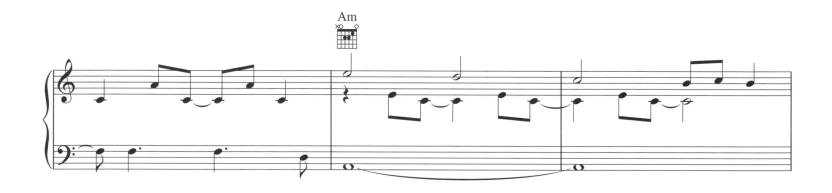

CAN'T FEEL MY FACE

Words and Music by ABEL TESFAYE,
MAX MARTIN, SAVAN KOTECHA,
PETER SVENSSON and ALI PAYAMI

19

EX'S & OH'S

Words and Music by TANNER SCHNEIDER
and DAVE BASSETT

HELLO

Words and Music by ADELE ADKINS
and GREG KURSTIN

32

HERE

Words and Music by ALESSIA CARACCIOLO, WARREN FELDER,
ISAAC HAYES, COLERIDGE TILLMAN,
ANDREW WANSEL, ROBERT GERONGCO,
SAMUEL GERONGCO and TERENCE LAM

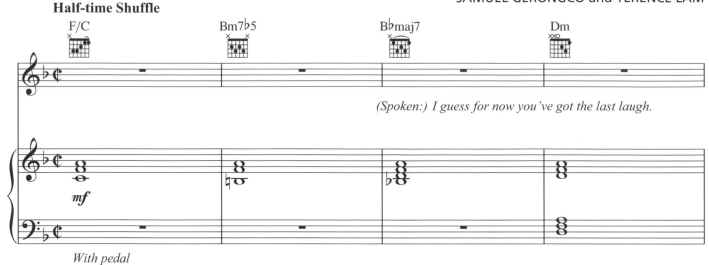

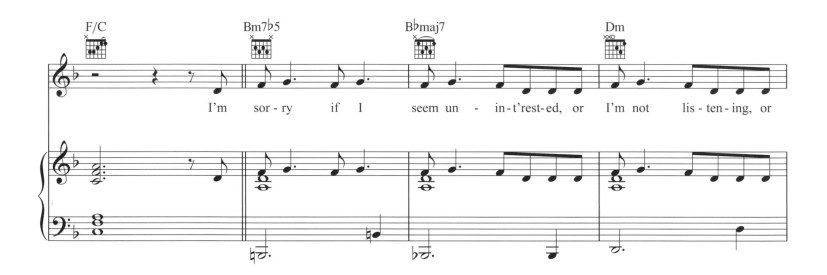

LET IT GO

Words and Music by JAMES BAY
and PAUL BARRY

Recorded a half step higher.

LIKE I'M GONNA LOSE YOU

Words and Music by CAITLYN ELIZABETH SMITH,
JUSTIN WEAVER and MEGHAN TRAINOR

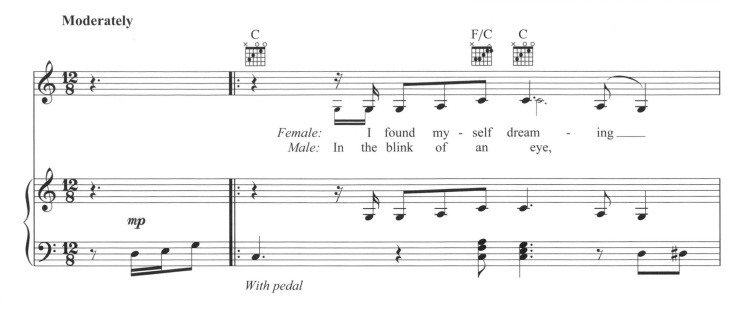

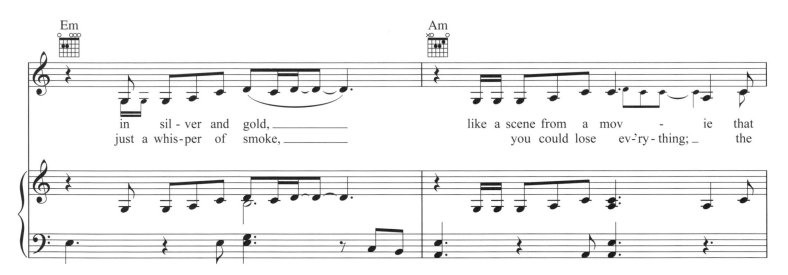

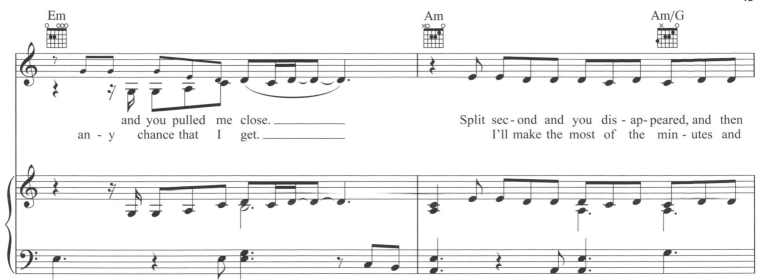

and you pulled me close. _____
an - y chance that I get. _____

Split sec - ond and you dis - ap - peared, and then
I'll make the most of the min - utes and

I was all a - lone. _____
love with no re - gret. _____

I woke up in tears with you by my side.
Let's take our time to say what we want,

Breath of re - lief, and I re - al - ized, _____
use what we've got be - fore it's all gone; _____

no, ___ we're not
'cause, no, _____ we're not

PERFECT

Words and Music by HARRY STYLES,
LOUIS TOMLINSON, JOHN HENRY RYAN,
JESSE SHATKIN, MAUREEN McDONALD,
JACOB HINDLIN and JULIAN BUNETTA

Moderate Pop Rock

I might nev-er be ___ your knight ___ in shin-ing ar- mor;
I might nev-er be ___ the hands ___ you put your heart ___ in

I might nev-er be ___ the one ___ you take home to moth- er;
or the arms that hold ___ you an - - y time you want ___ them.

and I might nev-er be ___ the one ___ who brings you flow- ers,
But that don't mean that we ___ can't live ___ here in the mo - ment,

LOVE YOURSELF

Words and Music by ED SHEERAN,
BENNY BLANCO and JUSTIN BIEBER

Moderate Ballad

For all the times ___ that you rained ___ on my ___ pa - rade, and all the clubs ___
___ me that you hat - ed ___ my friends, the on - ly prob -

___ you get in us - ing my name. ___ You think you broke ___
- lem was with you and not them. ___ And ev - 'ry time ___

___ my heart, oh, girl, for good - ness ___ sake. You think I'm cry -
___ you told me my o - pin - ion was wrong and tried to make ___

RENEGADES

Words and Music by ALEXANDER JUNIOR GRANT,
ADAM LEVIN, CASEY HARRIS, NOAH FELDSHUH
and SAM HARRIS

SHE USED TO BE MINE
from WAITRESS THE MUSICAL

Words and Music by
SARA BAREILLES

STITCHES

Words and Music by TEDDY GEIGER,
DANNY PARKER and DANIEL KYRIAKIDES

Recorded a half step lower.

STRESSED OUT

Words and Music by
TYLER JOSEPH

Shuffle groove

Rap 1: *(See additional lyrics)*

My name's Blur-ry-face, and I care what you think. My name's

us to sleep; but now we're stressed out. _____

We're stressed out. _____

Rap 2: *(See additional lyrics)*

"Wake up! You need to make mon-ey!" Yo.

Additional Lyrics

Rap 1:   I wish I found some better sounds no one's ever heard.
I wish I had a better voice that sang some better words.
I wish I found some chords in an order that is new.
I wish I didn't have to rhyme every time I sang.

I was told when I get older all my fears would shrink,
But now I'm insecure and I care what people think.

Rap 2:   Sometimes a certain smell will take me back to when I was young.
How come I'm never able to identify where it's coming from?
I'd make a candle out of it if I ever found it,
Try to sell it, never sell out of it. I'd probably only sell one.

It'd be to my brother, 'cause we have the same nose,
Same clothes, homegrown, a stone's throw from a creek we used to roam.
But it would remind us of when nothing really mattered.
Out of student loans and treehouse homes, we all would take the latter.

Rap 3:   We used to play pretend, used to play pretend, bunny.
We used to play pretend; wake up, you need the money.
We used to play pretend, used to play pretend, bunny.
We used to play pretend; wake up, you need the money.

We used to play pretend, give each other different names;
We would build a rocket ship and then we'd fly it far away.
Used to dream of outer space, but now they're laughing at our face,
Saying, "Wake up, you need to make money!" Yo.

WRITING'S ON THE WALL

from the film SPECTRE

Words and Music by SAM SMITH
and JAMES NAPIER

UMA THURMAN

Words and Music by ANDREW HURLEY, JOSEPH TROHMAN,
PATRICK STUMP, PETER WENTZ, JACOB SCOTT SINCLAIR,
LIAM O'DONNELL, WAQAAS HASHMI, JARRELL YOUNG,
JACK MARSHALL and BOB MOSHER

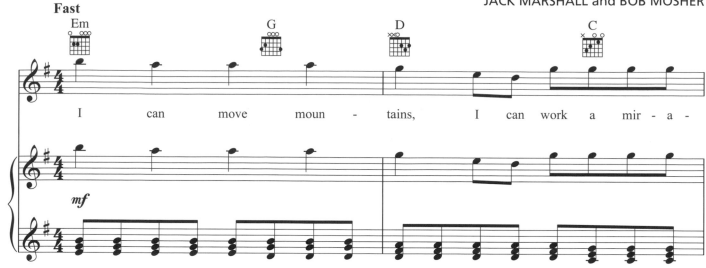

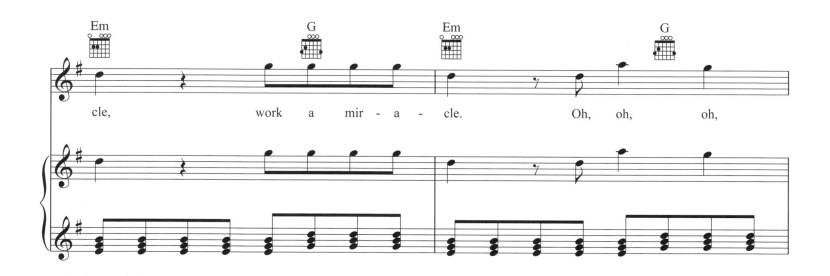

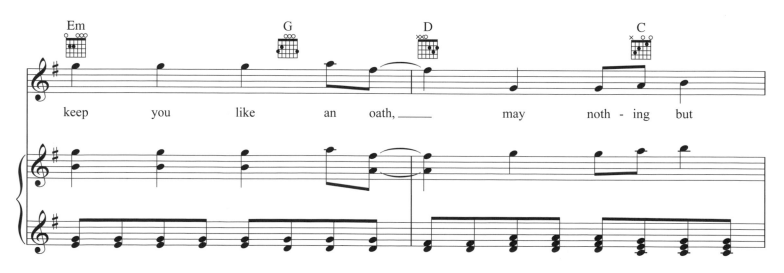

death   do   us   part.

She wants to dance   like

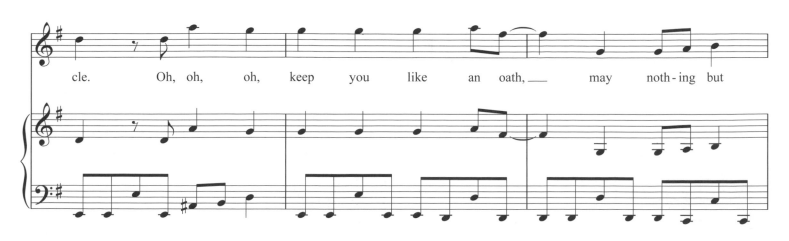

cle.   Oh, oh,   oh, keep you like an oath, ___ may noth-ing but

death   do   us   part.

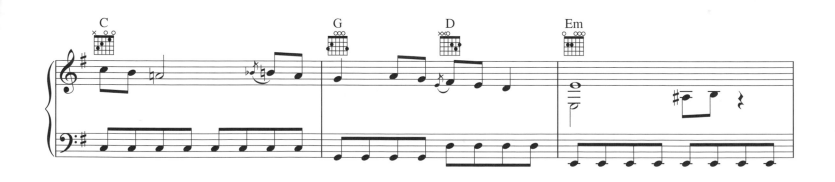

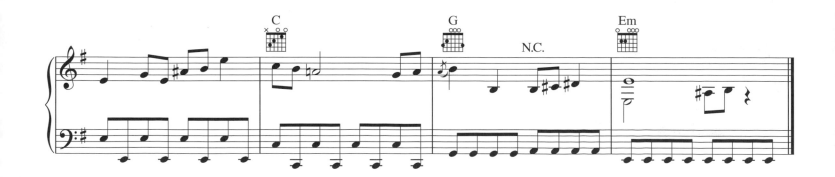

THE NEW DECADE SERIES

Books with Online Audio • Arranged for Piano, Voice, and Guitar

The New Decade Series features collections of iconic songs from each decade with great backing tracks so you can play them and sound like a pro. You access the tracks online for streaming or download. **See complete song listings online at www.halleonard.com**

SONGS OF THE 1920s
Ain't Misbehavin' • Baby Face • California, Here I Come • Fascinating Rhythm • I Wanna Be Loved by You • It Had to Be You • Mack the Knife • Ol' Man River • Puttin' on the Ritz • Rhapsody in Blue • Someone to Watch over Me • Tea for Two • Who's Sorry Now • and more.
00137576 P/V/G.........................$24.99

SONGS OF THE 1970s
ABC • Bridge over Troubled Water • Cat's in the Cradle • Dancing Queen • Free Bird • Goodbye Yellow Brick Road • Hotel California • I Will Survive • Joy to the World • Killing Me Softly with His Song • Layla • Let It Be • Piano Man • The Rainbow Connection • Stairway to Heaven • The Way We Were • Your Song • and more.
00137599 P/V/G $27.99

SONGS OF THE 1930s
As Time Goes By • Blue Moon • Cheek to Cheek • Embraceable You • A Fine Romance • Georgia on My Mind • I Only Have Eyes for You • The Lady Is a Tramp • On the Sunny Side of the Street • Over the Rainbow • Pennies from Heaven • Stormy Weather (Keeps Rainin' All the Time) • The Way You Look Tonight • and more.
00137579 P/V/G.........................$24.99

SONGS OF THE 1980s
Addicted to Love • Beat It • Careless Whisper • Come on Eileen • Don't Stop Believin' • Every Rose Has Its Thorn • Footloose • I Just Called to Say I Love You • Jessie's Girl • Livin' on a Prayer • Saving All My Love for You • Take on Me • Up Where We Belong • The Wind Beneath My Wings • and more.
00137600 P/V/G.........................$27.99

SONGS OF THE 1940s
At Last • Boogie Woogie Bugle Boy • Don't Get Around Much Anymore • God Bless' the Child • How High the Moon • It Could Happen to You • La Vie En Rose (Take Me to Your Heart Again) • Route 66 • Sentimental Journey • The Trolley Song • You'd Be So Nice to Come Home To • Zip-A-Dee-Doo-Dah • and more.
00137582 P/V/G.........................$24.99

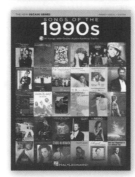

SONGS OF THE 1990s
Angel • Black Velvet • Can You Feel the Love Tonight • (Everything I Do) I Do It for You • Friends in Low Places • Hero • I Will Always Love You • More Than Words • My Heart Will Go On (Love Theme from 'Titanic') • Smells like Teen Spirit • Under the Bridge • Vision of Love • Wonderwall • and more.
00137601 P/V/G.........................$27.99

SONGS OF THE 1950s
Ain't That a Shame • Be-Bop-A-Lula • Chantilly Lace • Earth Angel • Fever • Great Balls of Fire • Love Me Tender • Mona Lisa • Peggy Sue • Que Sera, Sera (Whatever Will Be, Will Be) • Rock Around the Clock • Sixteen Tons • A Teenager in Love • That'll Be the Day • Unchained Melody • Volare • You Send Me • Your Cheatin' Heart • and more.
00137595 P/V/G.........................$24.99

SONGS OF THE 2000s
Bad Day • Beautiful • Before He Cheats • Chasing Cars • Chasing Pavements • Drops of Jupiter (Tell Me) • Fireflies • Hey There Delilah • How to Save a Life • I Gotta Feeling • I'm Yours • Just Dance • Love Story • 100 Years • Rehab • Unwritten • You Raise Me Up • and more.
00137608 P/V/G.........................$27.99

SONGS OF THE 1960s
All You Need Is Love • Beyond the Sea • Born to Be Wild • California Girls • Dancing in the Street • Happy Together • King of the Road • Leaving on a Jet Plane • Louie, Louie • My Generation • Oh, Pretty Woman • Sunshine of Your Love • Under the Boardwalk • You Really Got Me • and more.
00137596 P/V/G.........................$24.99

HAL•LEONARD® CORPORATION

7777 W. BLUEMOUND RD. P.O. BOX 13819 MILWAUKEE, WI 53213

halleonard.com

Prices, content, and availability subject to change without notice.

0415

THE BEST EVER

COLLECTION
ARRANGED FOR PIANO, VOICE AND GUITAR

100 of the Most Beautiful Piano Solos Ever
100 songs
00102787 .... $27.50

150 of the Most Beautiful Songs Ever
150 ballads
00360735 .... $27.00

150 More of the Most Beautiful Songs Ever
150 songs
00311318 .... $29.99

More of the Best Acoustic Rock Songs Ever
69 tunes
00311738 .... $19.95

Best Acoustic Rock Songs Ever
65 acoustic hits
00310984 .... $19.95

Best Big Band Songs Ever
68 big band hits
00359129 .... $17.99

Best Blues Songs Ever
73 blues tunes
00312874 .... $19.99

Best Broadway Songs Ever
83 songs
00309155 .... $24.99

More of the Best Broadway Songs Ever
82 songs
00311501 .... $22.95

Best Children's Songs Ever
102 songs
00310358 .... $22.99

Best Christmas Songs Ever
69 holiday favorites
00359130 .... $24.99

Best Classic Rock Songs Ever
64 hits
00310800 .... $22.99

Best Classical Music Ever
86 classical favorites
00310674 (Piano Solo) $19.95

The Best Country Rock Songs Ever
52 hits
00118881 .... $19.99

Best Country Songs Ever
78 classic country hits
00359135 .... $19.99

Best Disco Songs Ever
50 songs
00312565 .... $19.99

Best Dixieland Songs Ever
90 songs
00312326 .... $19.99

Best Early Rock 'n' Roll Songs Ever
74 songs
00310816 .... $19.95

Best Easy Listening Songs Ever
75 mellow favorites
00359193 .... $19.99

Best Folk/Pop Songs Ever
66 hits
00138299 .... $19.99

Best Gospel Songs Ever
80 gospel songs
00310503 .... $19.99

Best Hymns Ever
118 hymns
00310774 .... $18.99

Best Jazz Piano Solos Ever
80 songs
00312079 .... $19.99

Best Jazz Standards Ever
77 jazz hits
00311641 .... $19.95

More of the Best Jazz Standards Ever
74 beloved jazz hits
00311023 .... $19.95

Best Latin Songs Ever
67 songs
00310355 .... $19.99

Best Love Songs Ever
62 favorite love songs
00359198 .... $19.99

Best Movie Songs Ever
71 songs
00310063 .... $19.99

Best Pop/Rock Songs Ever
50 classics
00138279 .... $19.99

Best Praise & Worship Songs Ever
80 all-time favorites
00311057 .... $22.99

More of the Best Praise & Worship Songs Ever
76 songs
00311800 .... $24.99

Best R&B Songs Ever
66 songs
00310184 .... $19.95

Best Rock Songs Ever
63 songs
00490424 .... $18.95

Best Showtunes Ever
71 songs
00118782 .... $19.99

Best Songs Ever
72 must-own classics
00359224 .... $24.99

Best Soul Songs Ever
70 hits
00311427 .... $19.95

Best Standards Ever, Vol. 1 (A-L)
72 beautiful ballads
00359231 .... $17.95

Best Standards Ever, Vol. 2 (M-Z)
73 songs
00359232 .... $17.99

More of the Best Standards Ever, Vol. 1 (A-L)
76 all-time favorites
00310813 .... $17.95

More of the Best Standards Ever, Vol. 2 (M-Z)
75 stunning standards
00310814 .... $17.95

Best Torch Songs Ever
70 sad and sultry favorites
00311027 .... $19.95

Best Wedding Songs Ever
70 songs
00311096 .... $19.95

Prices, contents and availability subject to change without notice. Not all products available outside the U.S.A.

HAL•LEONARD® CORPORATION
7777 W. BLUEMOUND RD. P.O. BOX 13819 MILWAUKEE, WI 53213

Visit us online for complete songlists at

31901059868069

0615